DISCOVER THE **MOST AMAZING FIGHTING PLANES** ON EARTH!

MEGA BOOK OF
COMBAT
AIRCRAFT

www.alligatorbooks.co.uk

© 2006 Alligator Books Limited

Published by
Alligator Books Limited
Gadd House, Arcadia Avenue
London N3 2JU

Printed in China

CONTENTS

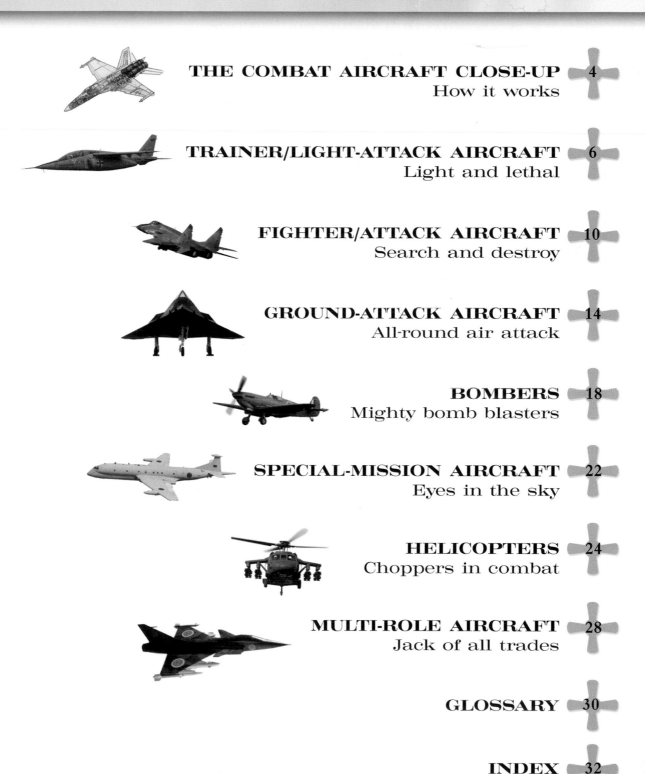

THE COMBAT AIRCRAFT CLOSE-UP 4
How it works

TRAINER/LIGHT-ATTACK AIRCRAFT 6
Light and lethal

FIGHTER/ATTACK AIRCRAFT 10
Search and destroy

GROUND-ATTACK AIRCRAFT 14
All-round air attack

BOMBERS 18
Mighty bomb blasters

SPECIAL-MISSION AIRCRAFT 22
Eyes in the sky

HELICOPTERS 24
Choppers in combat

MULTI-ROLE AIRCRAFT 28
Jack of all trades

GLOSSARY 30

INDEX 32

Long before the first flying machines took to the skies, the world relied on ships to carry troops and equipment across vast oceans. Indeed, many great wars were lost and won at sea. The invention of the aircraft also made it possible to fight from the air, adding an extra dimension to the battlefield. Today, many different aircraft are the striking forces of the world's major military powers, capable of deploying troops worldwide in a matter of hours! On the following pages you can read about some of the fastest and most powerful aircraft today.

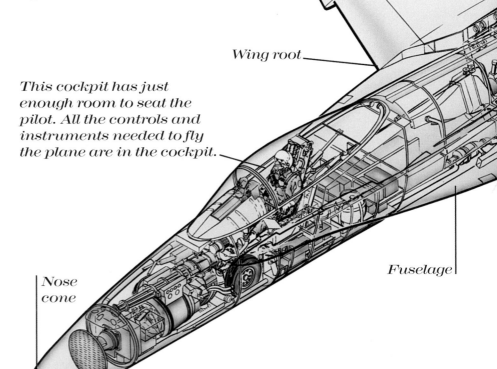

Wing root

This cockpit has just enough room to seat the pilot. All the controls and instruments needed to fly the plane are in the cockpit.

Fuselage

Nose cone

Turbojet Engine

How does a turbojet engine really work? First, air enters the front intake. A compressor compresses the air as it passes into the combustion chambers. Nozzles spray fuel into the chambers, and a spark ignites the air/fuel mixture. The gases that form expand and pass into the exhaust at the rear of the combustion chambers. The gases generate forward thrust as they escape to the rear. As the gases leave the engine, they pass through the turbine – fan-like blades that rotate the turbine shaft. This shaft rotates the compressor, bringing in a new supply of compressed air through the intake.

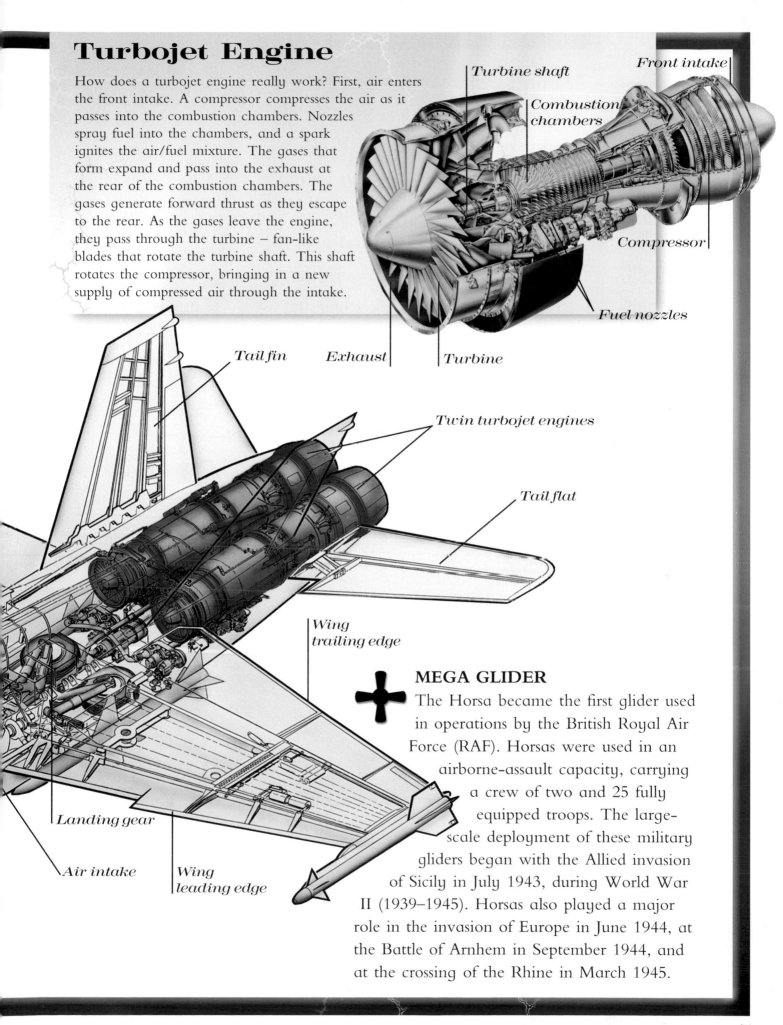

Turbine shaft

Front intake

Combustion chambers

Compressor

Fuel nozzles

Exhaust

Turbine

Tail fin

Twin turbojet engines

Tail flat

Wing trailing edge

Landing gear

Air intake

Wing leading edge

MEGA GLIDER

The Horsa became the first glider used in operations by the British Royal Air Force (RAF). Horsas were used in an airborne-assault capacity, carrying a crew of two and 25 fully equipped troops. The large-scale deployment of these military gliders began with the Allied invasion of Sicily in July 1943, during World War II (1939–1945). Horsas also played a major role in the invasion of Europe in June 1944, at the Battle of Arnhem in September 1944, and at the crossing of the Rhine in March 1945.

5

Military aircraft are used for a variety of tasks. Trainers take military officers through pilot-training programmes to make them rated aviators. Only rated military personnel can fly fixed- and rotary-wing military aircraft. Light attack aircraft are used for strategic attack and air interdiction, air defence, close air support, maritime missions, offensive counter-air missions and tactical reconnaissance. Modern light attack aircraft are capable of carrying a range of NATO-standard weapons, including Sidewinder air-to-air missiles (AAMs), air-to-ground missiles, rockets, free-fall bombs, laser-guided bombs and fuel drop tanks.

MEGA MISSIONS

During World War II, members of the Marine Corps aviation fighter squadron VMF-214, stationed on Espiritu Santo, an island in the South Pacific, engaged in some 1,766 individual missions (over 4,200 hours) in 84 days. During these missions, VMF-214 squadron destroyed 48 Japanese 'Zeros'.

EUROPEAN COLLABORATION

The twin-seat subsonic Alpha Jet was a joint venture between Dassault and Breguet in France and Dornier in Germany. Both countries wanted to produce a modern light attack, advanced trainer aircraft. The Alpha Jet E entered service in November 1977.

Zeppelin

The German Army had a fleet of seven Zeppelins in service when World War I broke out in 1914. These airships could fly at a maximum speed of 136 km/h at an altitude of 4,250 metres. Each Zeppelin carried 2,000 kilograms of bombs and were equipped with five machine guns. The first Zeppelin raid on London took place on 31 May 1915, killing 28 people.

✛ PEARL HARBOR

Just before 8am on 7 December 1941, Japan attacked the United States Pacific naval base Pearl Harbor in Oahu, Hawaii, while Japanese diplomats were holding 'peace talks' with US officials in Washington, DC. The surprise strike intended to cripple US military forces before they could join the Allies in World War II. The Japanese raid resulted in the loss of 2,403 members of the US armed forces, and 347 US aircraft and 21 US ships were destroyed or damaged. The Japanese Mitsubishi A6M Type 0 fighter aircraft, commonly known as the Zero, proved to be particularly successful in the attack on Pearl Harbor.

✛ AIR INTERDICTION

Air interdiction operations are distance strikes intended to delay enemy advances or destroy targets before the enemy poses a threat to friendly forces. Typical air-interdiction targets include enemy supply depots or transportation networks.

MEGA BOMB!

The very first bomb that Allied forces dropped on Berlin in World War II killed the only elephant in the Berlin Zoo.

ALPHA JET E

This light attack measures 12.3 metres in length, with a wing span of 9.14 metres and a height of 4.19 metres. It has two turbofan engines alongside the body under the wings, with a two-seat cockpit with a bubble canopy. The Alpha has a range of weapons capabilities and is particularly suitable as training craft and supporting aircraft for offensive operations. The military powers of Belgium, Cameroon, Egypt, France, Germany, Ivory Coast, Morocco, Nigeria, Portugal, Qatar and Togo all operate the Alpha Jet E.

HAWK 100

The Hawk family of aircraft was developed by British Aerospace and made famous by the 'Red Arrows' RAF Aerobatic Team. There are four configurations: the Hawk 50 series, including the Goshawk T-45 for the US Navy; the Hawk 60 series current production trainer aircraft; the Hawk 100; and the Hawk 200 single-seat, multi-role combat aircraft. The Hawk 100 series is an advanced two-seat weapons systems trainer with enhanced ground-attack capability. Short-range AAMs can be mounted on the wing tip missile launchers.

AERO L-159 ALCA

The Aero L-159 ALCA was developed to meet the Czech Air Force operational requirements for a light, multi-role combat aircraft. The capabilities of the L-159 include air defence, border patrol, close air support, tactical reconnaissance, lead-in fighter, maritime missions and weapons training. This aircraft has been designed to carry a range of NATO-standard weapons, including AIM-9L/M Sidewinder AAMs, AGM-65 Maverick air-to-ground missiles, free-fall bombs, fuel drop tanks, laser-guided bombs and rockets.

EADS MAKO

The Mako light attack, advanced trainer is a joint development between EADS in Germany and the armed forces of the United Arab Emirates. The testing phase for this aircraft started in 2003 and, if the test flights prove to be successful, the Mako should enter the production phase in 2007. Stealth technology has been incorporated into the design of the Mako, which has a single Eurojet EJ200 turbofan engine. The aircraft has seven hardpoints for external installation of weapons for anti-air and ground-attack missions, making it a truly awesome combat aircraft.

MEGA FACT

The Hawk family of aircraft are deployed by many military forces, including Brunei, Finland, Indonesia, Kenya, Kuwait, Malaysia, Oman, Saudi Arabia, South Korea, and the United Arab Emirates.

9

FIGHTER/ATTACK AIRCRAFT

Many of the latest technically advanced military aircraft are too expensive for some countries to buy in large quantities. Consequently, many of the aircraft manufactured during the Cold War are still in operation, especially by the military of non-NATO countries. For those air forces that cannot afford modern fighters and attack aircraft, upgrades to old aircraft seem the only choice.

WOODEN FIGHTER

The de Havilland Mosquito is considered by many experts to be one of the most important aircraft of World War II. This versatile light bomber was built almost entirely of wood due to limited supplies of aircraft-grade materials. The de Havilland Mosquito could fly at a maximum speed of 668 km/h – fast enough to dispense with defensive guns. The Mosquito Mk 1 prototype first flew in November 1940. Mosquitos marked targets in Germany for the RAF's Pathfinder night bombers. A few of the 7,781 built still fly as museum pieces today.

Erich Hartmann
'The Blonde Knight of Germany'

In the early days of aerial combat, pilots found it hard enough to shoot down just one aircraft without themselves being hit by enemy fire. But the Red Baron of Germany managed to shoot down a total of 80 aircraft during his time as a pilot in World War I. During World War II, 15 German pilots shot down 200 or more aircraft. But only one pilot reached 352. The name of this master aviator was Erich Hartmann, nicknamed 'The Blonde Knight of Germany'. On 8 May 1945, Hartmann set off on his final combat mission and downed aircraft number 352, a YAK7 fighter. Later that day, Hartmann landed his plane and surrendered to the British forces in the area.

FULCRUM FIREPOWER

The primary role of the MiG-29 Fulcrum is to destroy hostile air targets. For the purpose, this Russian Air Force fighter carries two BVR AA-10 'Alamo-As' inboard and four short-range AA-8 'Aphid' AAMs or AA-11 'Archer' IR-homing missiles outboard, backed by an internal 30 mm cannon and bombs weighing 3,000 kilograms.

SEEK AND DESTROY

The MiG-29 Fulcrum has an N-019 pulse-Doppler radar and a passive infra-red search and track (IRST) system. This can detect, track and engage a target while leaving the radar in non-emitting mode.

MIG-29 FULCRUM

The Moscow Air Production Organisation developed the MiG-29 Fulcrum for the Soviet Air Force to replace the MiG-21 and MiG-23 fighters for counter-air missions, as well as the Sukhoi Su-15 and Su-17 attack aircraft. Military engineers started designing the MiG-29 in 1974, and it took another three years before a prototype entered testing stages. The Fulcrum flies at a maximum level speed of 2,445 km/h with 3,000 kilograms of expendable stores, including rocket launchers and drop tanks on six external hardpoints. The Russian Air Force has recently started an upgrade programme for 150 MiG-29 Fulcrums – now designated MiG-29SMT.

FOCKE WULF FW 190

The German Focke Wulf Fw 190 was one of the greatest fighter aircraft of World War II. Designed by Dr. Kurt Tank, the prototype first took to the skies on 1 June 1939, after introductory ground tests. Although this aircraft was built as a sturdy all-round fighter, rather than a lightweight interceptor, the early Fw 190A-1 fighters were clearly superior to the British Supermarine Spitfire Mk V, and the RAF lost many aircraft when the FW 190A-1 finally entered service in the autumn of 1940.

Reconnaissance Aircraft

One of the most important missions of specialised air forces involves aerial reconnaissance and surveillance. These missions provide invaluable strategic information, enabling military planners to engage aerial fighter and bomber attacks on enemy air and surface forces and installations. The United States Air Force (USAF) U-2R is one such reconnaissance aircraft. The U-2R provides continuous day or night, high-altitude, all-weather, stand-off surveillance in direct support of US and Allied ground and air forces. The U-2R also provides images to the Federal Emergency Management Agency in support of disaster relief. The pilot needs to wear a full pressure suit due to the high altitude at which the U-2R operates.

BUCCANEER

The Buccaneer was originally designed for the Royal Navy to fulfil its requirement for a long-range carrier-based attack aircraft. After the Royal Navy retired all carrier aircraft, however, the Buccaneer was taken into service by the RAF. The Buccaneer first entered service for the Royal Navy in July 1962. From its first operational missions right up to the very last for the RAF in 1992, the Buccaneer remained one of the fastest low-level aircraft in any service, thanks in large part to the aircraft's high-thrust engine and small wings. Various nicknames have been given to the Buccaneer, including the Banana Bomber, Nana, Peeled Banana, Brick, Bucc, Easy Rider and Dirt Eater.

MEGA FACT
The Gloster Meteor was the only Allied jet fighter to see active service during World War II.

GROUND ATTACK AIRCRAFT

Aircraft armed with sophisticated 'stealth' radar technology and advanced digital avionics systems can drop a lethal cocktail of weapons on some of the most heavily fortified targets. During World War II, aircraft relied on clear visibility, good weather conditions and a perfect sighting of the target. With modern advances in aviation technology, ground attack aircraft can attack day or night, in poor weather and without even having to see their target.

✚ RADIO WAVES

In 1934, British scientist Sir Robert Watson Watt was part of a team studying radio reflections when he noticed a strange echo on his cathode ray tube. The echo turned out to be from a distant building. Once scientists realised that distant objects could be 'seen' using radio waves, it did not take long for the technology to be adapted for the military to track enemy aircraft and later to make air and sea navigation safer.

MEGA FACT
The German aircraft manufacturer Willy Messerschmitt first designed the classic Messerschmitt Bf 109 in 1935. More than 30,500 Messerschmitt Bf 109 aircraft were built before and during World War II.

Fearful Fighter

The Messerschmitt 163 Komet was the first operational rocket-propelled fighter, with a top speed of more than 950 km/h. The first Komet took to the skies in August 1941, carrying fuel for only 8 minutes of powered flight. The pilot glided into land, but the impact often caused residual fuel to explode, destroying the aircraft. The Komet took another three years before it entered active service. Had production started earlier, the Komet would have posed a huge threat to the Allies during the daylight bombing of Germany.

STEALTH ATTACK

The Lockheed Martin F-117A Nighthawk first entered service with the USAF in 1982. The unique design of this single-seat fighter/attack aircraft provides exceptional combat capabilities. The F-117A Nighthawk can employ a variety of weapons, including Paveway II and Paveway III armaments, and it is fitted with extremely sophisticated navigation and attack systems designed to pinpoint extremely well-defended targets.

MEGA FACT
The world's first operational swept-wing jet fighter was the Messerschmitt 262.

F-117A NIGHTHAWK

The F-117A Nighthawk is the world's first operational aircraft designed to exploit low-observable stealth technology. Lockheed Martin delivered 59 stealth fighters to the USAF between August 1982 and July 1990. During the 1991 Gulf War's Operation Desert Storm, between January and February 1991, the F-117A Nighthawk attacked the most heavily fortified targets in Iraq. Although only 36 stealth fighters were deployed to the region, accounting for just 2.5 per cent of the total force of 1,900 fighters and bombers, they flew more than a third of the bombing runs on the first day of the operation.

AV-8B HARRIER

The AV-8B Harrier has seen active service in the 1991 Gulf War during Operation Desert Storm, and it has also flown in a peace-keeping capability during the conflicts in Somalia and Bosnia. This aircraft can deliver an assortment of conventional stores, such as the CBU-99/100 Cluster Bomb Units, AIM-9L/M Sidewinder AAMs and anti-ship Harpoon and Sea Eagle missiles. In Operation Desert Storm, the AV-8B flew a staggering 3,380 sorties for a total of 4,083 flight hours.

AMX INTERNATIONAL

The main role of the AMX is for ground-attack operations in visual and marginal weather conditions. Other roles include air interdiction, close air support, reconnaissance and armed patrol. The AMX International has also proved effective in air-defence missions. A compact design, the AMX can operate from unprepared or partially damaged runways. Built as part of a joint European programme by Alenia, Aermacchi and Embraer, the AMX is used by the air forces of Brazil, Italy and Venezuela.

TORNADO GR1

The Tornado GR1 strike/attack aircraft first saw action in the 1991 Gulf War. (The aircraft can deliver a range of conventional stores.) For close air support and interdiction, the Tornado is equipped with iron bombs, cluster bombs and laser-guided bombs. In a defence-suppression role, it has anti-radar missiles, Sidewinder AAMs and twin internal 27 mm cannons. A mid-life update (MLU) programme saw 142 RAF Tornado GR1s planned for upgrade to Tornado GR4 configuration. The last of the updates was completed in 2003, ensuring that the Tornado serves well into the 21st century.

BOMBERS

The potential for aircraft to drop bombs on enemy targets was realised as early as 1911, when the first bombs were dropped during the conflict between Italy and Turkey. The first true bomber aircraft started life as scout planes during World War I, with the crew throwing grenades at enemy lines below. During World War II, bombers such as the German Gotha GIV carried up to 550 kilograms of bombs. Modern strategic bombers carry more than 22,000 kilograms of air-launched cruise missiles or conventional bombs.

SUPER SPITFIRE

The British Supermarine Spitfire series of fighter/bombers was built in increasingly fast and powerful versions, first with single RR Merlin 45 engines and later with the upgraded Merlin 60 engine series. Supermarine Aviation continually upgraded the Spitfire to meet all kinds of new demands, from low- and high-altitude fighters to an unarmed photo-reconnaissance aircraft.

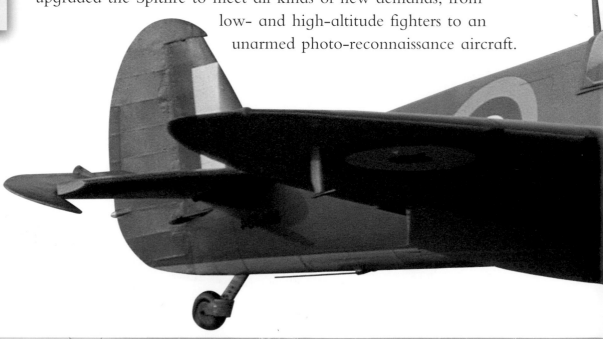

Bombs Away!

The payload and maximum speed of bombers rapidly increased during World War II. At the onset of the war, the German Heinkel He 111 had a bomb load capacity of 2,500 kilograms with a top speed of 405 km/h. By the end of World War II, however, the four-engine Avro Lancaster (shown right) had a bomb load capacity of 8,165 kilograms and could fly at a maximum speed of 462 km/h.

THE FLYING FORTRESS

The US Army Air Corps (USAAC) placed specifications for a multi-engine, anti-shipping bomber in 1934. Just one year later, Boeing Aircraft Company's Model 299 took to the skies on a test flight on 28 July 1935. Following evaluation and a series of re-designations, the first of a series of B-17 bombers was born. The final version, the B-17F or Flying Fortress, was introduced in September 1943. Most of the 8,680 Flying Fortresses built by Boeing bore the brunt of the US bomber efforts in Europe from 1944.

> **MEGA FACT**
> *The Convair B-36 Peacemaker was the largest bomber ever built. It first flew in 1946 and went on to serve as the US airborne nuclear deterrent in the early 1950s. The Peacemaker could carry the Mark 17 atomic bomb, which weighed a staggering 21 tonnes.*

SUPERMARINE SPITFIRE

The Supermarine Spitfire series served as front-line fighters throughout World War II and are some of the most famous military aircraft ever built. Spitfires were capable of flying at very high speeds due to the thin elliptical shapes of their wings. Wounded in the 1942 Battle of Britain, the Supermarine Spitfire series served in bomber, fighter, intercepter and reconnaissance roles in every major aerial combat during the war. Over 22,000 Spitfires and Seafires were built by Supermarine Aviation, but only a few remain in flying condition today.

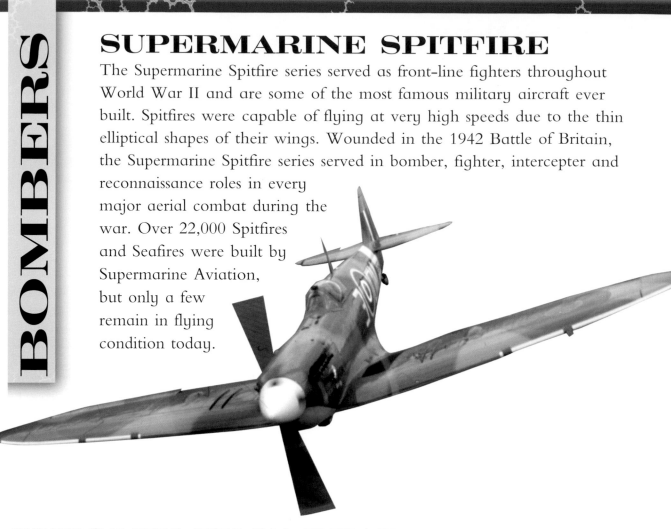

TUPOLEV TU-95 BEAR

The Tu-95 'Bear' heavy bomber was developed by the Soviet aircraft manufacturer Tupolev in the early 1950s. A prototype made its maiden flight on 12 November 1952, and the Russian Air Force hopes to see the current version, the Tu-95MS16, remain in service until 2015. The Bear is the first and only propeller-driven, swept-wing aircraft, and it is the fastest turboprop aircraft ever built. Travelling at a top speed of around 830 km/h, the Tu-95MS16 comes equipped with two AM-23 cannons in the tail turret, up to 16 cruise missiles and various conventional and nuclear weapons.

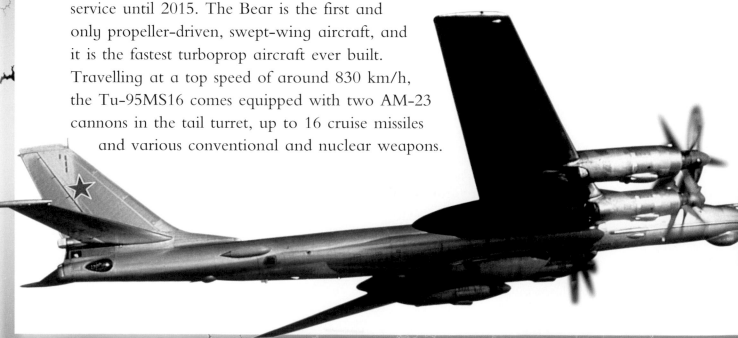

B-52H STRATOFORTRESS

The B-52H is the main nuclear bomber assigned to the Air Combat Command of the USAF. This long-range, heavy bomber can perform a variety of missions, flying at high subsonic speeds at altitudes of up to 15,240 metres. The B-52H can carry either nuclear or conventional ordnance with worldwide precision navigation capability. The jet bomber has eight TF33-P-3/103 turbofan engines arranged in four pairs, with large, flexible swept wings and a fuselage incorporating large bomb bays. B-52 aircraft have seen active combat in the Vietnam War (1954–1975) and the 1991 Gulf War.

B-2 SPIRIT

At the height of the Cold War, the US military decided to develop strategic bombers with nuclear capabilities to target the Soviet Union and other Eastern European countries. As well as being extremely fast, this new aircraft needed to be almost invisible to enemy sensors. The contractor, Northrop Grumman came up with the B-2 'Spirit', or 'stealth', bomber at a cost of billions of dollars. The B-2 has a wing span measuring a massive 52.1 metres, but to enemy radar scanners it is almost invisible. The exact mechanisms for the B-2's 'stealthiness' are classified, but the coating materials and flying wing design both appear to contribute to its low observability. The B-2 does not have any of the standard stabilising systems found on conventional aircraft, but this truly awesome bombing machine flies as smoothly as a fighter jet.

Special mission aircraft support conventional bomber and fighter operations by performing functions such as airborne early warning and control, suppression of enemy air defences, reconnaissance, surveillance and combat rescue.

NIMROD MRA4

British Aerospace based the Nimrod maritime reconnaissance aircraft (MRA) on the de Havilland Comet, combining the wings and fuselage of the Comet C4 with four turbofans and a long internal weapons bay beneath the existing fuselage. The first Nimrod's entered RAF service in 1969 and by 1998 all had been upgraded to MRA4 configuration.

S-3 VIKING

Lockheed Martin's S-3 Viking is the standard carrier-based, fixed-wing anti-submarine warfare (ASW) aircraft for the US Navy. The S-3 was developed to replace the Grumman S-2 Tracker ASW aircraft as a counter to the threat of a new generation of deep-diving, nuclear-powered Soviet submarines. The first of 179 S-3A Vikings entered service in 1975. The armament of the upgraded S-3B version includes Mk 82 free-fall bombs, Mk 53 mines, Mk 46 torpedos, Mk 36 destruction cluster bombs and flare launchers.

UCAV

The unpiloted combat air vehicle (UCAV) is a robot strike aircraft intended for use as a 'reusable cruise missile' in spearhead attacks on air-defence sites and other high-risk targets. UCAV missions would be conducted by an operator in a control aircraft, ground vehicle, warship or over a digital data link. The most advanced UCAV is Boeing's subsonic X-45A. The prototype was shown in September 2000, and the first test flight took place in 2001.

DASSAULT ATLANTIQUE

The first in the series of Dassault Atlantique aircraft, ATL1, entered service in 1966. This aircraft was selected as the NATO Long Range Maritime Patrol Aircraft and remains in service with the German, Italian and Pakistani navies. The ATL2 version has been in service with the French Navy since 1989. The ATL3 upgrade comes with an enhanced weapon system, new engines, a glass cockpit and sophisticated avionics and sensors. The primary mission of the Atlantique is anti-submarine and anti-surface warfare. Secondary roles include search and rescue, mine laying and detection and long-range maritime surveillance.

MEGA FACT
In 1962, Canberra PR9 reconnaissance aircraft were used to monitor the movements of Soviet ships during the Cuban missile crisis.

Helicopters were still in the early stages of their development during World War II, and they saw limited combat action. Britain and the Soviet Union did use them for observation purposes, but only in small numbers. Combat helicopters were not used on a large scale until the Vietnam War, when the US military realised the need for more aerial firepower and a way to provide armed escort for cargo-carrying choppers.

CHASED BY CHOPPERS!

By the end of the 1960s, the armies of most military powers had formed new air-combat units, with helicopters armed with anti-tank missiles such as the Tube-Launched, Optically-Tracked, Wire Guided (TOW) missiles. From this point on, helicopters became a vital piece of military hardware for the world's major armed forces.

THE AUTOGYRO

In 1923, the Spanish aeronaut Juan de la Cierva designed and constructed a primitive helicopter called the autogyro. This machine was more stable than the simple helicopter built by Louis-Charles Bréguet in 1917. From 1925 until the end of World War II, hundreds of autogyros were built in Europe and the United States.

Armed and dangerous

The Soviet Kamov Ka-50 single-seat (Ka-52 is a two-seater) close-support helicopter boasts an impressive array of weaponry. A 2A-42 gun is mounted on right side, fed with 500 rounds of 30 mm ammunition. The four pylons usually house 12 Vikhr laser-homing missiles or four 20-tube launchers for S-8 80 mm rockets. Other armaments include R-60 or R-73 AAMs; two Kh-25 MP anti-radiation missiles; FAB-250 or KAB-500Kr bombs; or 9A622 or 624 gun pods.

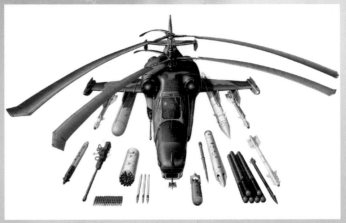

ENTER THE EUROPEANS

In June 1995, the armed forces in Greece became the first European military power to purchase the Apache. The Greek military now has a total of 20 AH-64As in service. The Apache is suitable for an all-weather anti-armour role both at day and by night.

MEGA FACT
By the end of the 1990s, there were approximately 26,500 civil and 29,700 military helicopters worldwide.

BRITISH SUCCESS STORY

The first successful British helicopter flew in 1938. The Weir W.5 was designed by C. G. Pullin, weighed 390 kilograms fully loaded and could fly at a top speed of 110 km/h. In 1939, the W.5 was upgraded to a version called the W.6, which was the first two-seat helicopter in the world.

AH-64A APACHE

The AH-64A Apache first took to the skies on 30 September 1975. This heavily armoured tandem attack/recce helicopter was developed for the US Army and proved to be extremely useful in Operation Desert Storm in 1991. The Apache can continue flying for at least 30 minutes after being hit by 12.7 mm bullets anywhere in the lower hemisphere. A total of 827 AH-64As were purchased by the US Army, with the final helicopters delivered in 1996.

KAMOV KA-52 ALLIGATOR

Using the NATO code name 'Hokum', the Ka-50 is the world's first single-seat, close-support helicopter. The pilot sits in a double-wall steel cockpit behind bullet-proof, flat-screen glazing. In an emergency, the K-37 ejection system explodes, separating the main rotor blades and cockpit roof. The pilot's seat is then dragged upwards and out of the helicopter by a rocket pack. A two-seat version called the Ka-52 'Alligator' first flew on 25 June 1997.

EUROCOPTER TIGER

The Franco–German Eurocopter 'Tiger' has been developed in three configurations: HAC (French) and UHT (German) anti-tank helicopters, and a combat support helicopter designated HAP for the French Army. In a combat support role, the Tiger uses a gun for short-range engagements, 68 mm rockets at medium and long range, and Mistral missiles to dispatch airborne threats. The Tiger comes equipped with a turreted 30 mm gun together with a combination of either four Mistral missiles, 44 rockets plus four Mistral missiles, or 68 rockets.

> **MEGA FACT**
> *The first true helicopter, in which the rotor serves both for propulsion and lift, was the VS-300 developed by Soviet-born US aeronaut Igor Sikorsky.*

CHINOOK CH-47

The medium lift CH-47 series of Chinook helicopters was developed in the Soviet Union, in 1956. They have been regularly upgraded ever since. These twin-engine, tandem rotor helicopters were designed for transporting cargo, troops, and weapons, both day and night. The Chinook is capable of delivering up to 10 tonnes of cargo or as many as 45 fully equipped soldiers in most battlefield environments.

> **MEGA FACT**
> *Designed in 1959 as a heavy assault troop carrier for the US Army, the CH-47 Chinook is the largest twin-rotor helicopter in service outside Russia.*

MULTI-ROLE AIRCRAFT

In addition to the conventional fighter/attack, bomber and specialised support aircraft, aviation forces deploy a number of multi-role aircraft with a wide range of capabilities, such as air defence, ground and sea attack, and reconnaissance roles.

SAAB JAS 9 GRIPEN

Aircraft requirements changed with the end of the Cold War, and many aircraft were no longer needed. Many of the next-generation aircraft, such as the all-purpose Swedish JAS 39 Gripen, can perform multiple tasks. Configuring the aircraft for attack, fighter or recce mission types is easily done by modifying onboard computer software and related systems.

DASSAULT RAFALE

The Rafale is a twin-jet, multi-role fighter capable of performing a range of missions, from air defence to nuclear strike deterrence. Developed for the French military, the Rafale can carry payloads of 9 tonnes on 14 hardpoints for the Air Force version and 13 for the naval version. The range of ordnance includes a 30 mm cannon, ASMP nuclear weapons, Mica AAMs and Exocet ASMs.

MEGA FACT

At the time of the Battle of Britain in 1942, the RAF had more Hawker Hurricanes than any other type of fighter aircraft.

F-16 FIGHTING FALCON

The Lockheed Martin F-16 Fighting Falcon can locate targets in almost all conditions. In an air-to-surface role, the F-16 Fighting Falcon can fly more than 860 km, deliver weapons with supreme accuracy, defend itself against enemy aircraft, and return to base. The USAF F-16 multi-mission fighters were deployed to the Persian Gulf in support of Operation Desert Storm in 1991. More F-16 sorties were flown than with any other US aircraft. These fighter aircraft were used to attack a variety of Iraqi targets, including airfields, Scud missiles sites and suspected military-production facilities.

MEGA FACT
The C-5 Galaxy is one of the world's largest aircraft. This heavy-cargo transporter can deploy any of the US Army's combat equipment, including the 66,600-kilogram mobile scissors bridge, helicopters and tanks.

MIRAGE 2000

The multi-role Mirage 2000 combat fighter has been in service with the French Air Force since 1984. The Mirage has nine hardpoints for carrying weapon-system payloads, such as the Magic 2, heat-seeking, air-to-air combat missiles and Super 530D semi-active AAMs with look-down and shoot-down capabilities. The Mirage is also equipped to carry a range of ASMs.

GLOSSARY

AAA   Anti-Aircraft Artillery

AAM   Anti-Aircraft Missile

AGM   Air-to-Ground Missile

ALCM   Air Launched Cruise Missile

ASW   Anti-Submarine Warfare

ATGM   Anti-Tank Guided Missile

CAP   Combat Air Patrol

CHOPPER   An informal term for a helicopter.

COCKPIT   The cabin at the front of an aircraft where the pilot and crew sit.

DOGFIGHT   Close combat between fighter planes.

FBW   Fly-By-Wire (the flight surfaces are controlled electronics, not mechanics).

FUSELAGE   The main body of an aircraft.

HARDPOINTS   Pylons or other fittings enabling missiles or other loads to be attached to an aircraft or helicopter.

HOTAS   Hands On Throttle And Stick

IFR   In-Flight Refuelling

LCD   Liquid Crystal Display

LGB   Laser Guided Bomb

MEGA FACT
In 1917, the French aviation pioneer Louis-Charles Bréguet built a prototype helicopter with four rotors.

LGW Laser Guided Weapon

LIFT The force that pushes an aeroplane up into the air.

LOH Light Observation Helicopter

RAF The Royal Air Force of the United Kingdom.

RECCE Reconnaissance mission

SAM Surface-to-Air Missile

SAR Sea And Rescue

SRAM Short-Range Attack Missile

STOL Short Takeoff and Landing

SUBSONIC Flying slower than the speed of sound.

SUPERSONIC Flying faster than the speed of sound.

THRUST The force that pushes an aeroplane through the air.

TURBOJET Gas turbine engine in which the exhaust gases deliver the thrust used to propel an aircraft through the air.

UHF Ultra High Frequency

USAF United States Air Force

VSTOL Vertical/Short Takeoff and Landing

WINGSPAN The distance between the wing tips of an aircraft.

MEGA FACT
In the years following World War I, Germany secretly trained and organised the Luftwaffe, since the 1918 Treaty of Versailles banned Germany from developing an air force.

INDEX

A

Aero L-159 ALCA 9
afterburners 4
AH-64A Apache 25, 26
air interdiction 7
airships, Zeppelin 7
Alpha Jet 6, 8
AMX International 17
Apache helicopters 25,
    26
Atlantique, Dassault 23
autogyros 24
AV8-B Harrier 16, 17
Avro Lancaster 18

B

B-2 Spirit 21
B-17F Flying Fortress
    19
B-52H Stratofortress 21
Bear, Tupolev Tu-95
    20
Boeing B-17s 19
bombers 18–21
bombs, atomic 19, 21
Buccaneer 13

C

C-5 Galaxy 29
Canberra PR9 23
Chinook CH-47 27
Cold War, end 10
Convair B-36
    Peacemaker 19

D

Dassault Atlantique 23
Dassault Rafale 28
de Havilland Mosquito
    10
Desert Storm,
    Operation 16, 21,
    26, 29
Devastator, Douglas
    TBD 8
Douglas TBD
    Devastator 8

EADS Mako 9
engines 4, 5
Eurocopter Tiger 27

F

F-16 Fighting Falcon
    29
F-117A Nighthawk 15,
    16
fighter/attack aircraft
    10–13
Flying Fortress 19
Focke Wulf Fw 190 12
Fulcrum, Mig-29 11,
    12

G

Galaxy, C-5 29
gliders 5
Gloster Meteor 13
Goshawk T-45 8
ground attack aircraft
    14–16
Gulf War (1991) 30
see also Desert Storm

H

Harrier, AV8-B 16, 17
Hartmann, Erich 11
Hawk aircraft 8, 9
Heinkel He 111 19
helicopters 24–27, 30
Horsa 5
Hurricane, Hawker 28

I

infra-red search and
    track system 11

K

Kamov Ka-50 and
    Ka-52 25, 26
Komet, Messerschmitt
    15

L

Lancaster, Avro 18

light attack aircraft 6–9
Lockheed Martin F-16
    Fighting Falcon 29
Lockheed Martin
    F-117A Nighthawk
    15, 16
Lockheed Martin S-3
    Viking 22

M

Mako, EADS 9
Messerschmitt 163
    Komet 15
Messerschmitt 262 15
Messerschmitt Bf 109
    14
Meteor, Gloster 13
Mig-29 Fulcrum 11, 12
Mirage 2000 29
Mosquito, de Havilland
    10
multi-role aircraft
    28–29

N

Nighthawk 15, 16
Nimrod MRA4 22
Nobel, Alfred 31

P

Peacemaker, B-36 19
Pearl Harbor 7
PR9, Canberra 23

R

radio waves 14
Rafale 28
reconnaissance aircraft
    13, 17
Red Baron 11

S

S-3 Viking 22
SAAB JAS 39 Gripen
    28
special mission aircraft
    22–23

Spirit, B-2 21
Spitfire, Supermarine
    18, 20
stealth aircraft
    B-2 Spirit 21
    F-117A Nighthawk 15,
    16
Stratofortress, B-52H
    21
Supermarine Spitfire 18,
    20

T

Tiger, Eurocopter 27
Tornado aircraft 17
Tupolev Tu-95 'Bear'
    20
turbine 5

U

U-2R 13
UCAVs 23
unpiloted aircraft 23

V

Viking, S-3 22
VMF-214 squadron 6
VS-300 27

W

Weir W.5 25
World War I 7, 11
World War II
    aircraft 10, 12, 13,
    15, 18, 19, 20
    Erich Hartmann 11
    first bomb used 7
    Pearl Harbor 7
    VMF-214 squadron
    6

X

X-45A 23

Z

Zeppelins 7
Zero, Mitsubishi 7, 8

Picture Credits

7, Philip Jarrett; 8 (bottom), Philip Jarrett; 9 (both), Mark Wagner/aviation-images.com; 10, Richard Napper;
11, Hulton|Archive; 12 (top), Richard Napper; 13 (bottom), Philip Jarrett; 15, Hulton|Archive; 17 (top), Philip
Jarrett; 22 (top), Philip Jarrett; 23 (top), Mark Wagner/aviation-images.com; 26 (bottom), Mark
Wagner/aviation-images.com; 27 (both), Phil Jarrett
All other pictures Alligator Books Limited.